Earthforms

Valleys

by Christine Webster

Consultant:
Robert S. Anderson, PhD
Associate Professor of Geological Sciences
University of Colorado at Boulder

Capstone press

Mankato, Minnesota

Bridgestone Books are published by Capstone Press,
151 Good Counsel Drive, P.O. Box 669, Mankato, Minnesota 56002.
www.capstonepress.com

Library of Congress Cataloging-in-Publication Data
Webster, Christine.
    Valleys / by Christine Webster.
    p. cm.—(Bridgestone books. Earthforms)
    Includes bibliographical references (p. 23) and index.
    ISBN 0-7368-3716-7 (hardcover)
    1. Valleys—Juvenile literature. I. Title. II. Series.
GB561.W43 2005
910'.914'4—dc22   2004014469

Summary: Describes valleys, including how they form, plants and animals on valleys, how people and
    weather change valleys, Death Valley, and the Great Rift Valley.

Editorial Credits

Becky Viaene, editor; Juliette Peters, designer; Anne McMullen, map illustrator; Ted Williams,
    illustrator; Wanda Winch, photo researcher; Scott Thoms, photo editor

Photo Credits

Corbis/Catherine Karnow, 16; Steve Kaufman, 10; Sygma/Ponti/Grazia Neri, 12
Corel, 1
Getty Images/Derek Croucher, cover
James P. Rowan, 4, 14, 18
Photo courtesy of Jack Hursh, 8

1 2 3 4 5 6 10 09 08 07 06 05

Table of Contents

What Are Valleys? 5

How Do Valleys Form? 7

Plants in Valleys .9

Animals in Valleys 11

Weather Changes Valleys 13

People Change Valleys 15

Death Valley 17

Great Rift Valley 19

Valleys on a Map 21

Glossary 22

Read More 23

Internet Sites .23

Index 24

What Are Valleys?

Valleys are deep grooves in the earth's surface. They are low areas of land between two higher areas. The valley bottom is called a floor. Valley sides are called walls or slopes. Rivers run through most valleys.

Valleys are like canyons. Both have low land between two areas of higher land. Valleys are found between two hills or mountains. Canyons are found between two very steep cliffs.

◄ McDonald Creek runs through a valley in Montana's Glacier National Park.

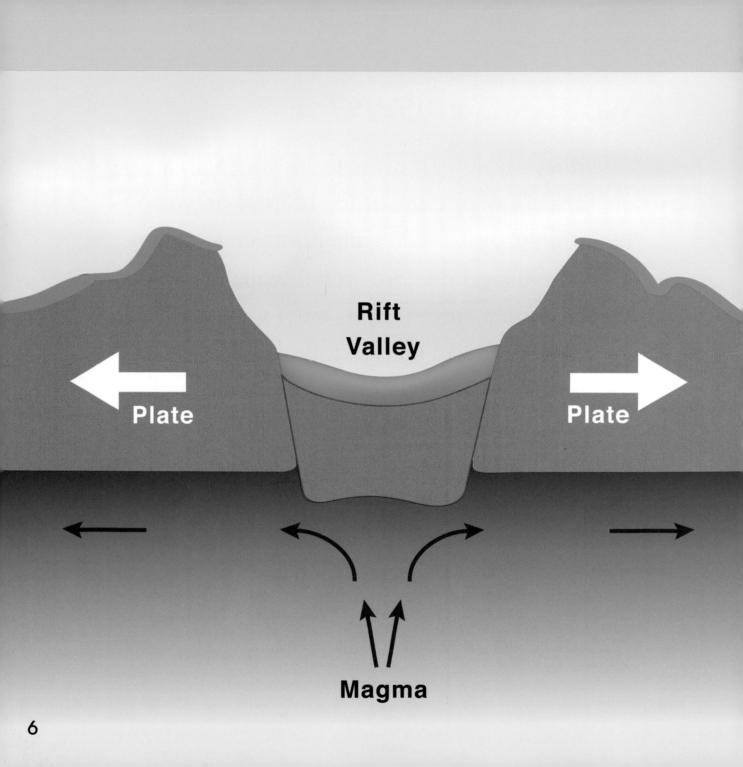

How Do Valleys Form?

Most valleys are created by **erosion**. Rain runs down mountains and hills. The rain flows into rivers. Rivers cut V-shaped valleys into the land.

Glaciers create U-shaped valleys. Glaciers erode both the sides and bottoms of an area to form a valley.

Earth's movements also form valleys. Huge rocky plates make up earth's outer shell. The plates pull apart and drop into **magma**. A rift valley is left in the middle.

◄ Rift valleys form when two of earth's plates pull apart.

Plants in Valleys

Climate affects what types of plants grow in valleys. In mild climates, wild flowers bloom alongside birch and willow trees.

Fewer plants grow in hot, dry valleys. Cactus and desert holly can grow in these climates. In some valleys, no plants can grow. The climate is too hot and dry.

◄ Lupines and other wild flowers add color to a valley in Nevada.

Animals in Valleys

Climate also affects what animals can live in each valley. Many different animals live in valleys with mild climates. Red-winged blackbirds and meadowlarks fly in valley skies. Bears search for food on valley floors. Turtles, frogs, beavers, and fish swim in valley rivers.

Not many animals can live in hot, dry valleys. Mice, coyotes, and bighorn sheep do live in California's hot Death Valley.

◄ Grizzly bears are often seen in the valleys of Alaska's Denali National Park.

Weather Changes Valleys

Each year, rain causes valley walls to erode a little further. When it rains, small pieces of valley walls are washed down to the valley floor. Heavy rains cause walls to erode quickly, making the valley floor wider.

Rain and melting snow can also change the soil of a valley floor. Melting snow and heavy rains can fill a valley river. The river overflows onto a **floodplain**. When the flooding stops, rich soil is left behind.

◄ Heavy rains overflow a valley's river, flooding a road on a valley floor in Piedmont, Italy.

14

People Change Valleys

People live in many valleys. Animals leave valleys when cities and towns are built in them. Natural plants are cleared from valleys for farming and roads.

Sometimes people try to control rivers in a valley. They build high walls beside rivers to prevent flooding.

Some valleys are in national parks. National parks are protected from people. People can't change valleys in national parks.

◄ Many people farm and live in valleys of the Andes Mountains near Cotopaxi, Ecuador.

Death Valley

California's Death Valley is the lowest valley in North America. It drops 282 feet (86 meters) below **sea level**. It is about 140 miles (225 kilometers) long.

Death Valley is also the driest and hottest valley in North America. Death Valley gets about 2 inches (5 centimeters) of rain each year. Summer temperatures can soar past 120 degrees Fahrenheit (49 degrees Celsius).

◄ People walk on salt flats in Death Valley. They formed after a large lake dried up and left salt behind.

18

Great Rift Valley

One of the largest cracks on the earth is the Great Rift Valley. This valley was formed by movement of the earth's plates. The Great Rift Valley is more than 4,000 miles (6,438 kilometers) long. It reaches across almost the entire length of Africa. Some Great Rift valley walls are over 6,000 feet (1,829 meters) high.

The world's longest **freshwater** lake is inside the Great Rift Valley. Lake Tanganyika is 410 miles (660 kilometers) long.

◀ Farmland spreads across parts of the Great Rift Valley in Kenya, Africa.

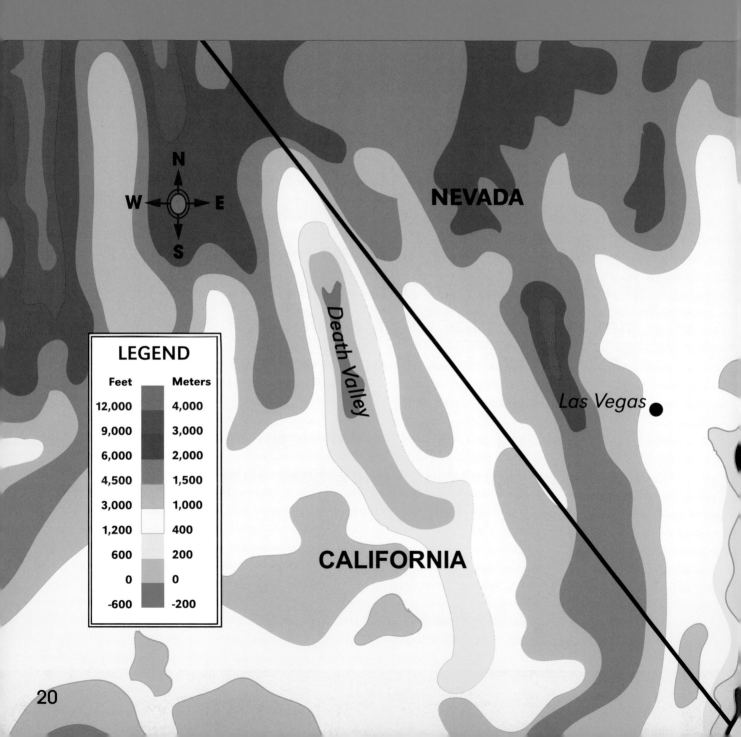

Valleys on a Map

The deepest area of a valley can be found on an **elevation** map. On these maps, different colors show different elevations.

People can use hiking maps to explore valleys. Hikers use maps to find valley rivers. They may also see animals on hiking trails. Maps help people learn more about valleys.

◄ Three green colors show the difference of elevation between the floor and walls of Death Valley.

Glossary

climate (KLYE-mit)—the usual weather in a place

elevation (el-uh-VAY-shuhn)—the height above sea level; sea level is defined as zero elevation.

erosion (i-ROH-zhuhn)—a slow wearing away of soil and rock by water and wind

floodplain (FLUHD-plane)—an area of low land near a stream or river that floods during heavy rains

freshwater (FRESH-wa-tur)—water that does not have salt

glacier (GLAY-shur)—a huge moving body of ice found in mountain valleys or polar regions

magma (MAG-muh)—melted rock that is found beneath earth's surface

sea level (SEE LEV-uhl)—the average level of the ocean's surface; sea level is a starting point from which to measure height or depth.

Read More

Brimner, Larry Dane. *Valleys and Canyons.* A True Book. New York: Children's Press, 2000.

Salzmann, Mary Elizabeth. *In a Valley.* What Do You See? Edina, Minn.: Abdo, 2001.

Internet Sites

FactHound offers a safe, fun way to find Internet sites related to this book. All of the sites on FactHound have been researched by our staff.

Here's how:
1. Visit *www.facthound.com*
2. Type in this special code **0736837167** for age-appropriate sites. Or enter a search word related to this book for a more general search.
3. Click on the **Fetch It** button.

FactHound will fetch the best sites for you!

Index

animals, 11, 15, 21

canyons, 5
climate, 9, 11, 17

Death Valley, 11, 17, 21

erosion, 7, 13

floodplains, 13
formation, 7, 17, 19

glaciers, 7
Great Rift Valley, 19

Lake Tanganyika, 19

magma, 7
maps, 21

national parks, 5, 11, 15

people, 15, 21
plants, 9, 15
plates, 7, 19

rain, 7, 13, 17
rift valleys, 7, 19
rivers, 5, 7, 11, 13, 15, 21

sea level, 17
snow, 13

U-shaped valleys, 7

valley floors, 5, 11, 13, 21
valley walls, 5, 13, 19, 21
V-shaped valleys, 7

weather, 13